Political & Economic Systems

DICTATORSHIP

Richard Tames

Heinemann
LIBRARY

www.heinemann.co.uk/library
Visit our website to find out more information about Heinemann Library books.

To order:

 Phone 44 (0) 1865 888066

Send a fax to 44 (0) 1865 314091

 Visit the Heinemann Bookshop at www.heinemann.co.uk/library to browse our catalogue and order online.

First published in Great Britain by Heinemann Library,
Halley Court, Jordan Hill, Oxford OX2 8EJ,
a division of Reed Educational and Professional Publishing Ltd.
Heinemann is a registered trademark of Reed Educational and Professional Publishing Ltd.

OXFORD MELBOURNE AUCKLAND
JOHANNESBURG BLANTYRE GABORONE
IBADAN PORTSMOUTH (NH) USA CHICAGO

Designed by AMR
Originated by Dot Gradations
Printed in Hong Kong by South China Printing

ISBN 0 431 12431 0
06 05 04 03 02
10 9 8 7 6 5 4 3 2 1

British Library Cataloguing in Publication Data

Tames, Richard
  Dictatorship. – (Political & economic systems)
  1. Dictatorship – Juvenile literature
  I. Title
  321.9

Acknowledgements
The publishers would like to thank the following for permission to reproduce photographs:
Bridgeman: p. 25; Bridgeman/British Museum: p. 17; Corbis/Archivo Iconografico: p. 24; Corbis/Bettmann: pp. 20, 28, 32, 40, 42; Corbis/Bill Gentile: p. 11; Corbis/Charles Lenars: p. 16; Corbis/Christel Gerstenberg: p. 35; Corbis/David and Peter Turnley: p. 53; Corbis/Sygma/Lundt Dimitri: p. 44; Corbis/Sygma/Robert Patrick: p. 50; Hulton Archive: pp. 6, 8, 26, 31, 37; Kobal Collection: p. 21; Rex: p. 45.

Cover photograph: Supporters of Saddam Hussein, reproduced with permission of Associated Press.

Every effort has been made to contact copyright holders of any material reproduced in this book. Any omissions will be rectified in subsequent printings if notice is given to the publishers.

Our thanks to Christopher Gibb for his comments in the preparation of this book.

◯ Contents

1   The Night of the Long Knives   4

2   What makes a dictatorship?   7

3   Styles of dictatorship   10

4   The origins of dictatorship   22

5   Fascism and its friends   31

6   What dictatorships achieve   39

7   How dictatorships end   49

8   So, what is dictatorship?   55

Timeline   56

Further reading, sources and websites   58

Some 20th-century dictators   59

Glossary   61

Index   64

Any words appearing in the text in bold, **like this**, are explained in the glossary.

① The Night of the Long Knives

On 29 June 1934, dozens of tough-looking men wearing brown uniform shirts gathered from all over Germany at a hotel in the lakeside resort of Bad Wiesee. Respectable Germans disliked them as rowdy bullies, but they were also afraid of them. They were members of the **SA – Sturmabteilung** ('Storm Troopers') – the **Nazi** party's **militia**. The Nazi party under Adolf Hitler had been the government of Germany since January 1933. SA men strutted the streets, drilled and practised with weapons and looked forward to ever more power in the new Nazi Germany.

The SA's top commander, Ernst Röhm, had launched Hitler's political career. He was confident of Hitler's support for his plan to absorb the regular German army into the SA, with himself in command. Röhm could not have been more wrong. Hitler saw the SA as too big and dangerously out of his direct control. He now wanted to work with the professional armed forces to rearm Germany and to win the support of respectable Germans in making the country prosperous again.

Hitler arrived unexpectedly early at Bad Wiesee on the morning of 30 June 1934. Röhm and the other top SA leaders were still asleep. They were immediately disarmed, arrested and taken away by Hitler's personal bodyguard, black-uniformed **SS – Schutzstaffel** ('defence squadron') men, to Nazi party headquarters in Munich, where they were shot. There were other executions without trial throughout the country. Not all of these were SA men. Others were political opponents it was convenient to get rid of as part of the same operation.

It was announced that Röhm had been planning to seize power for himself. It was officially admitted that eighty-seven plotters had been killed. The real number was probably hundreds. Newspapers were forbidden to publish details of the victims and all documents connected with 'the measures taken on 30 June, 1 and 2 July' were destroyed, so no one could be sure. On 4 July, at a special ceremony, Hitler personally presented each SS executioner with a special dagger to honour their loyalty to him. On 13 July he told the

German Reichstag (parliament), 'If any one ... asks why I did not turn to the regular courts ... then all I can say to him is this: in this hour I was responsible for the fate of the German people and thereby I became the supreme judge on behalf of the German people ... I gave the orders to shoot the ringleaders in this treason ...'

Leaders of the world's **democracies** were as horrified to hear Hitler's claim that he stood above the law as they were at his open use of murder. But among ordinary German people there was widespread approval. They believed the faked-up evidence of a plot and applauded Hitler's merciless action against the alleged plotters. Germany's generals were pleased to see SA plans to take over the military ended. Germany's leading law professor, Carl Schmitt of Berlin University, praised Hitler's direct justice.

Less than a month later, Germany's aged president, Paul von Hindenburg, died. Hitler then simply merged the vacant position of president with his own post of chancellor (prime minister) and made himself commander-in-chief as well, with the single title of Führer (leader). All officers, soldiers and government officials from then on were made to swear a personal oath of loyalty and obedience to Adolf Hitler, the Führer of the German Reich and German People. Hitler had shown that even those who thought they were his loyal supporters were not safe from his **arbitrary** power. He had taken one more decisive step towards making himself dictator – sole master – of Europe's biggest nation.

Forms of **dictatorship** can be traced back to ancient Greece, but Adolf Hitler ranks with Joseph Stalin of the Soviet Union and Mao Zedong of China as an example of the new sort of dictator made possible by technology in the 20th century.

Hitler at the microphone. He spent many hours rehearsing, not only his own speeches but also the dramatic gestures that accompied them.

The styles of government they created are known as **totalitarian** because they aimed at total control over the people they governed. No aspect of ordinary people's lives – the friends they had, what they read, how they passed their leisure time – was considered to be a purely private matter, outside politics. Dictators have always had the negative aim of crushing opposition to their rule. In modern times they have also had the positive aim of transforming the country they governed.

Sayings of the dictators

Adolf Hitler
'I learned the use of terror from the communists, of slogans from the Catholic church and the use of **propaganda** from the democracies.'
'The greater the lie, the greater the chance it will be believed.'
'With us the Leader and the Idea are one and every party member has to do what the leader orders.'
'In starting and waging a war it is not right that matters, but victory.'

Joseph Stalin
'We are fifty or a hundred years behind the advanced countries. We must make good this distance within ten years. Either we do it or they crush us.'
'A single death is a tragedy: a million is a statistic.'

Mao Zedong
'Political power grows out of the barrel of a gun.'
'A revolution is not a dinner party or writing an essay or doing embroidery. A revolution is an act of violence ...'

② What makes a dictatorship?

Adolf Hitler's ruthless treatment of his own supporters on the Night of the Long Knives shows a number of the key features of a modern **dictatorship**.

Concentration of power

Decision-making is in the hands either of a single dictator or of a small committee. There are no legal checks and balances against the abuse of power except the failure of the system to act efficiently itself. This can happen when the dictator rewards loyal followers with jobs that they are too corrupt or incompetent to carry out, or when they work against each other to increase their personal power.

Arbitrary rule

The **constitution**, if there is one, is largely meaningless in practice. Laws are either ignored or misapplied. There is no effective **rule of law**. **Secret police** operate outside the law to spy on and destroy any opposition. Dictatorships readily and routinely use violence to repress opposition by imprisoning or murdering their opponents or driving them into **exile**. But dictatorships cannot be based on violence and repression alone. At the very least they need the obedience of the police, armed forces or party **militia** they rely on to use violence against their opponents.

A ruling ideology

An **ideology** is a set of ideas which explains a political programme. **Democracies** tolerate differing ideas about both the methods and aims of politics, but dictatorships force people to accept a single ideology. This is the officially approved view of what political action ought to achieve and what methods should be used to achieve it. Other aims and methods are suppressed. The main instrument for imposing an ideology is usually a political party led by the dictator. Normally it is the only permitted party, but is often supported by other organizations, such as a militia, youth movement, or a women's section.

Mussolini in Fascist Party uniform hails an adoring crowd. Many dictatorships have been genuinely popular and needed little force to maintain themselves in power. Mussolini's rousing speeches excited and flattered his followers into believing they were building a great new future for Italy.

Core supporters

Winning the active support of at least part of the general population limits the need to use violence and is essential for stability. Depending on the country concerned, crucial groups of supporters might include large landowners, trade unions, tribal chiefs, students or religious institutions.

In the 20th century, dictatorships usually wanted much more than mere obedience, aiming to get the bulk of the population involved in carrying out political programmes, such as redistributing land, building up industry or expanding the armed forces.

Successful dictatorships have recruited positive supporters to serve as party officials, **militia** officers and so on and rewarded them with well-paid jobs and influence in the system. They also gained more passive, less committed support from groups which benefited from their rule. These benefits may be material, such as land, jobs, healthcare or education, or they may be psychological, like pride in one's country or race, expulsion of a foreign ruler, overthrow of a cruel government, defeat of a hated enemy or order and stability after a period of chaos.

Throughout the 20th century, democracy and dictatorship were rivals as systems of government. Perhaps surprisingly, democracy has had the better of it. This did not look likely in Europe in the 1920s, when **fascism** was on the rise, or in the 1950s, when **communism** seemed to spread through every continent, or in the 1970s, when many newly independent countries in Asia and Africa lurched between dictatorship and chaos. Fascism was smashed by defeat in World War II. With the break-up of the **Soviet Union** in 1989–91 communism collapsed there and in eastern Europe, and was weakened where it had been imitated in Asia. Throughout Asia, Africa and Latin America dictatorships have given way to democracies, although that trend has been uneven and sometimes reversed.

Explaining their politics

Fascism
'Fascism is a religion: the 20th century will be known as the century of fascism.'
'For the fascist, everything is in the state and nothing human or spiritual exists, much less has value, outside the state.'
'Fascism believes that permanent peace is neither possible nor useful.'
Benito Mussolini

'A creed entirely given over to hate, to irreverence and to violence.'
Pope Pius XI

Nazism
'We must develop organizations in which an individual's entire life can take place. Then every activity and every need of every individual will be regulated ... by the party ... there are no longer any free realms in which the individual belongs to himself ... The time of personal happiness is over.'
Adolf Hitler

Communism
'The theory of communism may be summed up in one sentence : Abolish all private property.' Karl Marx and Friedrich Engels
'Communism has nothing to do with love. It is an excellent hammer which we use to destroy our enemy.' Mao Zedong

③ Styles of dictatorship

Many **dictatorships** have had the outward trappings of democratic government – a **constitution**, elections, newspapers, even **demonstrations**. But in a dictatorship these do not affect how the political system actually works – through corruption, force, fraud, terror and trickery.

Democracies have a more or less family resemblance to one another. They are based either on the British 'Westminster model' of parliamentary government or some variant form of the American or French presidential **republics**. Dictatorships, by contrast, developed in many guises, though often borrowing techniques of government from one another.

The **fascist regimes** of Italy (1922–43) and Germany (1933–45) and their imitators and allies before and during World War II were based on the idea of an inspired man of destiny, who could transform his nation by winning the eager, disciplined support of the people.

The more backward-looking *caudillismo* of Latin America and Spain continued the 19th-century traditions of the rule of a strong man. *Caudillos* were supported by the armed forces and by the Roman Catholic church in the interests of order and stability. Sometimes they borrowed the outward style of fascism, in terms of such things as party uniforms, **propaganda**, youth movements and mass rallies, but they usually aimed to keep things as they were rather than bring about great changes.

In 1973 Argentina's former dictator, Juan Péron, returned from exile to be freely elected as president but died the following year after failing to tackle the country's economic problems. In 1976 the military seized power, banned all political parties and carried on a 'Dirty War' against any opponents who dared to challenge its rule. About 15,000 people 'disappeared' and must be presumed dead. In 1982, to distract Argentines from their problems, the **junta** leader General Galtieri ordered the invasion of the British-occupied Falkland Islands, which Argentina had long claimed as its own.

FOR MORE INFORMATION ON PÉRON AND PINOCHET, SEE PAGES 59–60.

For a few weeks the military were popular, but when Britain recaptured the islands Galtieri was forced from power and civilian rule was restored.

Chilean military dictator Augusto Pinochet (with sash) reviews a military parade. From the 1960s onwards a new form of dictatorship emerged in Latin America, in which senior officers, supported by well-disciplined and old-established armed forces and aided by technocrats, seized power to solve an economic crisis or crush extremist movements.

Communist states theoretically aimed to free the mass of ordinary people and offer them a better life in a more just society. In practice they repressed them through the use of **secret police**, **militias** and party and state officials. Sometimes dictatorial power in communist states was in the hands of small committees of party officials, sometimes power was exercised by a single individual. Some communist states lasted for half a century or more. Others, like Colonel Haile Mariam Mengistu's in Ethiopia (1977–91), called themselves communist but failed to establish lasting regimes because they were constantly at war with their opponents or with neighbouring countries.

Africa and Asia have thrown up a wide range of regimes in former European **colonies**, which from the 1940s onwards became independent countries. They have varied greatly in what they claimed to represent and in the degree of bloodshed and chaos they caused. There have been two main types of dictatorship.

The first is the **civilian** system. This is based on a single ruling political party, headed by a **charismatic** politician, often the leader of the movement for national independence. A good example was Kwame Nkrumah (1909–72), ruler of Ghana from its independence in 1957 to his overthrow by the army in 1966.

The second type of dictatorship is the military regime. This is based on newly-established armed forces and often headed by a junior, or at least a newly promoted and inexperienced officer, for example Idi Amin, dictator of Uganda from 1971 to 1979.

Both types of dictatorship have often been split by conflicts between different tribes, regions or ethnic or religious groups. Both have tended to become purely personal systems of rule, which have proved incapable either of delivering effective government or of building strong regimes which would outlast the dictator himself. These systems of personal rule might genuinely try to turn a political vision into reality, such as transforming a poor agricultural country into a modern industrial one. But many simply became robber regimes, treating the state as the private property of the dictator, to be used for his personal benefit and to buy the loyalty of such people as favoured generals, party bosses and business leaders.

Dictators and monarchs

Although dictatorship was known in the ancient world, it only became common from the 19th century onwards. For most of human history states have been governed by **monarchs** – with titles such as 'king', 'tsar', 'shah', 'sultan', 'rajah' or 'emperor'. Unlike modern dictators, monarchs rarely based their claim to rule on their personality or the need to carry out some political programme. Normally a king had to be of royal blood. He was usually the son or brother of the previous ruler or at least chosen by him, and was often confirmed in office by a coronation ceremony or some form of acceptance by a council of powerful nobles or priests. Although some kings did act like modern dictators in ruling by terror or ordering the killing of their opponents, most accepted limits to their power. These were usually set by law, custom or religion. Kings acknowledged that even they were subject or answerable to some higher power, usually divine. Unlike kings, who usually inherit their position, dictators have to justify their right to rule by claiming to be extraordinary men or promising to do extraordinary things.

A bust of the young Roman emperor Caligula (ruled AD 37–41). Occasionally traditional monarchs behaved as arbitrarily as modern dictators. Rulers whose cruelty seemed totally arbitrary, like the Roman emperors Caligula or Commodus (ruled AD 180–92) – both of whom came to believe that they actually were gods – usually ended up being murdered, often by their own bodyguards.

13

Machiavelli – principles or power ?

From the 14th century onwards, Italy came to resemble ancient Greece in being divided into a number of contending city-states, which were frequently at war with one another. Some were ruled by princes. Others were **republics** in form, but were ruled in practice by the head of a powerful family who was a prince in everything except the actual name. Florence was run by the fabulously rich Medici family for three centuries. They became celebrated as generous patrons of poets and painters, who often glorified them in return.

These princely rulers were known as **despots**. Like modern dictators, they wanted to concentrate power in their own hands and were constantly on guard against rivals, whom they were prepared to imprison or even murder. Like modern dictators, they often claimed to be ruling for the benefit of their people and justified their personal power by saying that it was necessary to guard against foreign enemies. Unlike modern dictators, however, they had no ambition to control the lives of their subjects in detail, providing they were content to stay out of politics. Unlike modern dictators, also, they had to at least pretend to respect Christian teachings and the authority of the Church.

From the Middle Ages, many handbooks had been written to tell rulers how they should govern. Almost all were written by churchmen, who naturally declared that rulers should follow the teachings of the Church and be truthful, generous, just and merciful. *The Prince*, written by Niccolo Machiavelli (1469–1527) in 1513, was quite different and brutally realistic. Machiavelli had worked for the republican government of Florence until it was overthrown in 1512. He lost his job and used his enforced retirement to write about what he had learned. Machiavelli knew from first-hand experience that real Italian politics was full of blackmail, betrayal and murder. His starting-point was his own rather low opinion of human nature, 'One can make this generalization about men: they are ungrateful, fickle, liars and deceivers, they avoid danger and are greedy for profit ...'

Machiavelli wrote at a time when Italy had been invaded by both French and Spanish armies and reduced to a battleground. As an Italian who wanted to see the foreigners driven out and order restored, Machiavelli hoped that a strong and ruthless leader would emerge to do the job. The main purpose of *The Prince* is to show such a man how to gain power and, having gained power, how to use it and keep it. The most important quality a ruler needed was what Machiavelli called *virtu*, which can be translated as 'guts' or 'nerve', the willingness to do what needs to be done in an uncertain world of unseen threats, sudden dangers and unpredictable crises.

Machiavelli warned rulers against being cruel for pleasure and advised them to make their subjects prosperous and contented. He knew that anyone with power has enemies as a matter of course, but it would be foolish to add to their number without good cause. But when it was essential to act there should be no holding back, 'The injury done to a man ought to be such that you do not need to fear his revenge'.

Models for Machiavelli

Some scholars believe that Machiavelli had the career of Cosimo de Medici (1389–1464) in mind when he was writing about the perfect prince. Cosimo used a fortune made from banking to bribe his way to power in Florence. He kept up the pretence that it was a republic, but packed all positions of power with his trusted supporters who constantly renewed his right to rule as a dictator. In theory his powers were purely temporary, but in practice they were permanent. Cosimo also used his money to hire troops from the Sforza family of Milan, thus freeing himself from the need to keep the Florentines personally loyal. Cosimo ruled Florence from 1434 until his death. The Medicis ruled Florence almost continuously until 1737.

Machiavelli also certainly knew and admired Cesare Borgia (1475–1507), the illegitimate son of Pope Alexander VI, who made him an archbishop when he was only seventeen. A brilliant lawyer, Cesare proved an equally outstanding commander of the Pope's army, conquering large parts of central Italy. He definitely had his own brother-in-law murdered and executed army commanders who plotted against him, but he lost his power when his father died, probably from poison.

Machiavelli knew that rulers are faced with life and death decisions which ordinary citizens do not face. Therefore, to stay in power, they had to do things which would be quite wrong for a private individual because, 'Politics have no relation to morals'. But Machiavelli also realized that appearance and reality are two different things and a prince should try at least to look like a good man, 'He should appear to be merciful, faithful to his word, kind, straightforward and religious ... But his character should be such that if he needs to be the opposite he knows how ... a prince, and especially a new prince, cannot observe all those things which give men a reputation for virtue, because in order to defend his state he is often forced to act against good faith, kindness, charity or religion ... so he should be flexible .., he should not depart from what is good, if that is possible, but he should know how to do evil, if that is necessary.'

Machiavelli's frankness made his name a byword for wickedness. Deceit, betrayal, plotting and assassination came to be denounced as ' Machiavellian'. Some thinkers, however, believed that Machiavelli should be praised for writing about politics as it really was, not as it ought to be.

The possibilities of power

The power of traditional monarchies to harm or even interfere much with the lives of their ordinary subjects depended on the resources and technologies they could command. Only the richest rulers had permanent armies. Most had to rely on forces supplied by powerful nobles or subject peoples, either of whom might revolt if treated too badly. Travel was usually difficult and often dangerous. Warfare was largely seasonal, rarely happening in winter. Politics concerned only a tiny élite. The mass of the population was unquestioningly loyal to the king unless actually driven to revolt. Nobody liked paying the taxes which the king used to pay his soldiers, judges and officials but most people valued a strong monarchy to defend them from invaders and punish banditry.

Traditional monarchies were supported by religious **ideologies**. Christianity, Islam and Buddhism all taught that the world was ordered by a divine power, represented on earth by rulers who governed righteously if they upheld religion and its teachings. Obedience to religion in this life would be rewarded in the afterlife.

What modern dictatorships can set out to do and the ways they can rule are far less limited than the opportunities which faced traditional monarchs. Industrialization has hugely increased the wealth available to governments to create mass **literacy** and employ vast numbers of officials, armed forces and police. The clock-based timetable, the typewriter and the telephone made it possible to regulate and control in detail the lives of the mass of citizens.

A powerful limit on rulers' ambitions has been weakened by the decline in religious belief. If people no longer believe in the supreme importance of life after death they may be more eager to follow a leader who promises them power and prosperity in their life on earth. Modern ideologies, such as communism and fascism, are future-looking but claim to transform life now for the better. Communist

A sixpenny piece bearing the head of Elizabeth I, looking suitably grand and dignified. Until very recently, most people never saw their ruler, except, perhaps as a face on a coin.

17

Allah's will

In the Islamic world some governments base their right to rule on the claim that they are enforcing Allah's laws.

In 1979 the rule of the shah (king) of Iran was overthrown by a mass movement led by the country's religious leaders. The Islamic republic they created has an elected parliament, but its laws and decisions are subject to review by the chief Ayatollah ('Sign from Allah'), an expert in Islamic law, who rules whether or not they conform to Allah's wishes.

Saudi Arabia is a monarchy, but claims to have no constitution except the Qur'an, the holy scripture of Islam. It also has no parliament, political parties or voters. The king, guided by Islam, rules by decree.

Afghanistan was ruled from 1994 to 2001 by the extremist Taliban ('Seeker') movement which enforced a cruel code of conduct on ordinary people, based on a crude version of Islam which ignored the interpretations and teachings of the religion's learned scholars. Women were entirely forbidden to go to school or work. Men were beaten if they did not grow long beards. TV, music and sport were banned. Rather than being based on religion, the Taliban government was simply based on force and its rules were rejected by the Afghan people as soon as its power to use violence was broken.

dictatorships set out to destroy the power of organized religion. They closed churches, seized church property, imprisoned priests and used the school system to attack religious beliefs. The Nazis treated Christianity as though it was out of date and irrelevant. They even tried to develop a **pagan** alternative, based on ancient German gods and legends. In fascist Italy, where the Roman Catholic church was too powerful to ignore, Mussolini used its fear of communism to limit its criticisms of his rule. On the whole, the church accepted fascism as better than chaos or communism.

New technologies

New technologies have given dictators the power to use violence on a whole new scale. In the past, mobs of rebellious peasants armed with farmyard tools often defeated regular soldiers, at least for a while, but would be easily **massacred** by professional troops with armoured vehicles and rapid-firing weapons. Ivan the Terrible ruled Russia brutally from 1547–84 and was responsible for killing thousands who rebelled against his rule. But he could only enforce his will through men riding on horses, armed with swords and primitive guns.

A portrait of Ivan the Terrible. Comparatively few of his subjects would have known what he looked like during his reign – this impression of him was painted by the Russian artist Viktor Vasnetsov nearly 350 years later.

Joseph Stalin, dictator of the **Soviet Union** from 1928 to 1953, used police forces and **militias** with machine-guns and artillery, trucks and tanks and railways, to wipe out millions of peasants who opposed his land reforms. He did this either by mass murder or he created famines by cutting off food supplies to whole regions.

New technologies of communication have brought the rulers and the ruled much closer together. Cheap printing, photography, radio and film have enabled rulers to communicate directly with their people. The subjects of Ivan the Terrible might never have seen him even once in their lifetime, but the citizens of Soviet Russia saw Stalin's face everywhere in newspapers and magazines, on posters and in school textbooks. Every town had a statue of him. Every year tens of thousands of people marched in great parades in front of him in person, but tens of millions could feel part of these events thanks to radio and cinema newsreels.

Stalin's purges

Lenin's death in 1924 was followed by a power struggle from which Stalin emerged as victor by 1928. He then introduced a series of Five Year Plans intended to transform the USSR into a modern industrial nation and bring all farming under state control. By simply taking land from the richer peasants (*kulaks*) and confiscating grain from the rest, Stalin caused a famine which killed over 6,000,000 people.

In 1934 Stalin ordered the murder of Sergei Kirov, a local comunist leader in Leningrad whose popularity he took as a threat to his own position. Kirov's death was then used as a pretext for the arrest and trial of hundreds and then thousands of loyal communists on trumped up charges of terrorism, plotting or sabotaging industry. The 'purge' of suspected traitors was then extended to the armed forces, leading to the execution or imprisonment of 35,000 officers. By 1938 about 8,000,000 people had been arrested and just under 7,000,000 people had been sent to camps as slave labour to build roads, dams, factories and power supplies. Less than 3% survived the standard ten year sentence. When Stalin died in 1953, there were still 12,000,000 prisoners in labour camps.

A nightmare vision

The English **socialist** George Orwell (1903–50) wrote his novel *Nineteen Eighty-four* immediately after World War II, when the full horrors of Nazism were being revealed and the communist USSR, under Stalin, was taking over the former democracies of eastern Europe.

In *Nineteen Eighty-four*, the world is divided into three empires, constantly at war with each other. The permanent crisis of war enables the Party, headed by Big Brother, to justify its complete power by claiming ever-present dangers from traitors and enemies which require the constant use of torture and terror. Every home is fitted with viddy-screens so the government can spy on everyone all the time. Children are rewarded for betraying their parents to the Thought Police if they say anything against the Party or Big Brother. There is no right to privacy, there is no such thing as private life, there are no rights. Everyone must dedicate their life to the Party and positively love Big Brother.

The hero of *Nineteen Eighty-four*, Winston Smith, is a victim of the system that oppresses him and everyone else outside the leadership of the Party. He is employed at the Ministry of Truth, constantly rewriting history so that no one can challenge the Party's complete control of information. This control is strengthened by the spread of Newspeak, a deliberately simplified form of English designed to end free thought by destroying the power to make contrasts or distinctions. In Newspeak, the words 'wrong', 'illegal', 'immoral', 'wicked' and 'evil' are replaced by the all-purpose term 'doubleplusungood'.

When Winston Smith falls in love, he challenges the whole system and must pay the price. He is tortured until he will agree that two plus two makes five and believes that they do so, until he will not only obey the Party but actually loves Big Brother – and does so sincerely.

A still from a film version of *Nineteen Eighty-four* made in 1984. The book was written as a warning, rather than a prophecy, a picture of what could happen, not what inevitably would.

The origins of dictatorship

Dictatorship is essentially a modern form of government, but it has had forerunners in the past that have inspired some of its forms and features. Modern dictators have sometimes been inspired by the example of great historical figures of the ancient world, like Julius Caesar, or military adventurers like Oliver Cromwell and Napoleon Bonaparte.

Ancient Greece

Greek thinkers recognized an oppressive form of one-man rule. They called it **tyranny**. The tyrant either ignored the law and seized power by force of arms, or inherited his position from someone who had. Because tyranny usually rested on the personal qualities of the tyrant – ambition, toughness, military skill, courage, ruthlessness – tyrannical rule often ended with the death of the tyrant or the overthrow of a successor too weak to hang on to power. Tyranny therefore was thought of as a form of rule that was basically unstable.

Tyrants were also installed by foreign powers, such as Persia and Macedonia, to rule conquered Greek city-states on their behalf. These tyrannies could last longer because the power of the tyrant depended less on personal qualities than on the use of foreign troops to suppress opposition.

Greek thinkers saw that in some situations tyranny might have value, such as bringing order after war or helping to make a change-over from rule by a small aristocracy to a more **democratic** form of government. Individual tyrants were sometimes great builders or generous patrons of artists and poets. But more often tyrants abused their power and acted cruelly, so the Greeks generally came to disapprove of tyranny.

Rome

Dictatorship in the early Roman **republic** was almost the opposite of what it became in the 20th century. It arose from emergency situations, such as the need to suppress a rebellion, but it was a legal position, intended to last for only a limited time.

The dictator was given complete power by the senate, Rome's supreme law-making body, but only for a maximum of six months. Any abuse of power might be punished afterwards by the law.

The ambitious Roman general Sulla (138–78 BC) got himself appointed dictator in 82 BC after a civil war and used his power to have dozens of political opponents murdered. By packing the senate with his supporters, he got it to declare his actions legal. This later inspired another ambitious general, Julius Caesar (c.102–44 BC). He was also appointed dictator after a civil war and then dictator for life. When he had his head put on the coinage, like a king, members of the old aristocracy which controlled the senate saw that Caesar was turning his position into a **monarchy**. They murdered him to preserve the republic, thus starting another, even worse, civil war which destroyed republican government completely.

France – crises in contrast

In the early stages of the French Revolution, when a republic had just been established, it was threatened by anti-revolutionary armies of **exiles** along its borders. Thousands of prisoners, accused of being enemies of the revolution in France, were **massacred** without trial. The revolutionary government came under the control of a fanatical lawyer, Maximilien Robespierre (1758–94). Like a Roman dictator defending the state in an hour of crisis, he continued the Reign of Terror until French victories ended the crisis.

In 1958 the French Fourth Republic collapsed over the future of Algeria, a French **colony** fighting for its independence. Party leaders appealed to retired war hero General Charles de Gaulle (1890–1970), liberator of France from **Nazi** occupation, restorer of democracy and, briefly, first post-war head of government. As a man above politics, he was asked to take power and rescue France from the risk of a military coup or even civil war. De Gaulle used his position to draw up a **constitution** for a new Fifth Republic with greatly strengthened powers for the President, a position de Gaulle himself held until 1969. He thus played the role of a Roman-style dictator, using temporary powers to re-establish constitutional government, rather than to end it.

This portrait of Robespierre shows him as a calm, well-groomed lawyer, but he was thought to be a wild fanatic. He was himself denounced for aiming at a personal dictatorship and guillotined without trial.

Soldiers of fortune

In medieval Europe successful kings were warriors, usually commanding the army in person. Most nobles were trained as fighting men and peasants were expected to defend their homes. During the 16th century, full-time professional armies came into being. This created the possibility that an ambitious general could use his army to seize power for himself.

Oliver Cromwell (1599–1658)

The abolition of the British monarchy in 1649 after the civil war and the execution of Charles I was followed by political confusion. Oliver Cromwell became a military dictator, because he could find no other way to govern, although he tried different systems. He refused the offer of the crown but did live in a palace, put his head on the coinage and took the title 'Lord Protector of the Commonwealth'. Cromwell's conquests brought the entire British Isles under one ruler for the first time, but he failed to provide for a successor. On his deathbed Cromwell chose his son Richard to succeed him, but Tumbledown Dick (as he was nicknamed) had been kept out of politics and was just ignored. Another former general, George Monck (1608–70), arranged to restore the monarchy and was royally rewarded for it. Cromwell remained a unique figure in British history, inspiring no further imitators as military dictator in Britain.

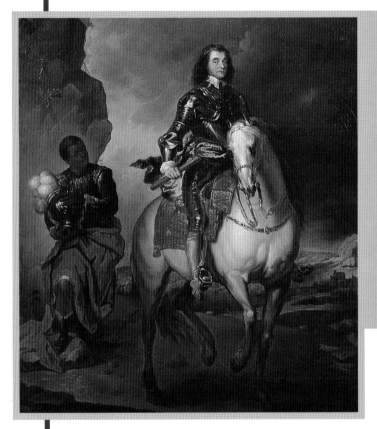

This portrait shows Cromwell as a royal figure, much like the king he had executed. Cromwell was an obscure, unambitious English country gentleman until civil war (1642–49) showed his unexpected talent as a commander of the victorious Parliamentary army.

Napoleon Bonaparte (1769–1821)

Unlike Cromwell, Napoleon was a professional soldier from his youth. He was also intensely ambitious. His military brilliance and the extraordinary opportunities created by the French Revolution made him an army commander at the age of just 26. Napoleon soon turned military glory into political power by becoming first a member of the government, then leader of the government for life, then crowning himself emperor (1804). As emperor he gave

France the code of laws still in force today and conquered most of Europe before being finally defeated and dying in exile, a prisoner of the British.

Napoleon's extraordinary career inspired his nephew, Louis-Napoleon (1808–73) to a life of conspiracy and exile until he, too, managed to come to power under a French republic. He imitated his uncle by overthrowing the republic to put himself on the throne of a Second Empire (1852–70). This, too, was smashed by military defeat by Prussia in 1870, and Napoleon III died in exile in Britain.

Caudillismo

Simon Bolivar (1783–1830) was dictator successively of Venezuela, Colombia and Peru. He aimed to give each country republican governments. He failed in his hope of bringing all the Spanish-speaking states of the region into a single unit along the lines of the USA. Bolivia, formerly Upper Peru, became a separate state, named in his honour.

An idealized portrait of Simon Bolivar shows him as a fearless and inspiring front-line commander. Noble by birth and a lawyer by training, Bolivar led the armies which freed the colonies of South America from Spanish rule.

Bolivar's career inspired many imitators, most of them with far less noble motives. In the 1820s the newly independent countries of Latin America were in much the same position as **post-colonial** states in Africa in the 1960s – rich in resources, but poor in educated manpower. National unity was held back by poor communications and ethnic divisions.

Many countries fell under the rule of *caudillos*. Some controlled a whole country, others only a region – but in Latin America a region might be as big as Belgium or Denmark. In many cases the *caudillos* relied on private armies, recruited from the peasants who worked their vast estates, to enforce their will. Juan Manuel de Rosas (1793–1877) raised a private army to seize power in Argentina, ruling by terror until his overthrow (1852). He then escaped to exile in England. In Paraguay, Francisco Solano López (1827–70) modelled himself on Napoleon and provoked a catastrophic five-year war against Brazil, Uruguay and Argentina. It took Paraguay two generations to recover from it.

Full-scale wars between states were relatively rare in Latin America, so in many countries the underemployed military were tempted to interfere in politics. Once established, the pattern of change of government by *golpe* (coup) and rule by a ***junta*** (council) of military commanders, occurred repeatedly. Since winning independence from Spain in 1825, Bolivia has had over sixty revolutions and eleven constitutions. Chile and Uruguay were unusual in developing as stable republics controlled by **civilian** politicians, changing power through peaceful elections.

Offspring of war

In terms of world politics 19th century Latin America was a blind alley. It was largely isolated from the rest of world and mostly free from foreign interference. Modern communications, however, have had the effect in the 20th century of making the politics of different states and regions affect one another much more. Countries trade with partners on opposite sides of the world. Large armed forces can operate thousands of miles from their home bases as they can be transported and supplied almost anywhere. Information travels almost instantaneously. The result has been a growing instability which has often destroyed political systems, opening the way to dictatorships.

World War I (1914–18) destroyed the empires of Russia, Germany, and Austria-Hungary, leading to the emergence of the **communist** USSR, **fascist** Italy and **Nazi** Germany. Fascist Italy and Nazi Germany in turn helped create General Franco's **regime** in Spain (1939–75) and various puppets and imitators in World War II.

Mao Zedong proclaims the establishment of the People's Republic of China in 1949. China then helped communists come to power in North Korea and North Vietnam.

FOR DETAILS ON MAO AND SOME OTHER DICTATORS, SEE PAGES 59–60.

A world apart

Albania's mountainous landscape hinders communications. This enabled its people to defeat invasion by Fascist Italy and helped Enver Hoxha to cut them off from the outside world.

Hoxha rose to power in the Albanian National Liberation Movement, formed with the aid of Tito's Yugoslav partisans. Declaring Albania a People's Republic in 1946, Hoxha made himself prime minister, foreign minister, defence minister and head of the communist party. His government took control of all farming and industry and banned both Christianity and Islam to make Albania the world's only officially atheist state.

Taking aid from the USSR and then China, Hoxha eventually quarrelled with both for not being communist enough, leaving Albania isolated even in the communist world. In 1973, 1974, 1975 and 1982 Hoxha had alleged enemies within the government and Albanian Communist Party removed from power and imprisoned or shot. Albania meanwhile became Europe's poorest country.

Communist control broke down after Hoxha's death in 1985, leading to widespread crime, food shortages and mass-unemployment, worsened by an influx of ethnic Albanian refugees from neighbouring Kosovo. Thousands of Albanians have since fled abroad in search of a better life, while unstable governments at home struggle to undo the damage of half a century's isolation.

World War II enabled the USSR to install communist dictatorships throughout eastern Europe. Enver Hoxha (1908–85) of Albania and Marshal Josip Tito (1892–1980) of Yugoslavia used their anti-fascist **partisan** armies to set up communist dictatorships after the war.

By weakening the overseas empires of Britain, France and the Netherlands, World War II hastened the independence of their colonies. The new states were often weak and could not control corruption or ethnic, religious or tribal conflicts. Neither could they cope with economies based on a few crops or raw materials whose world price could rise and fall unpredictably. Corruption, conflict and chaotic prices create conditions in which the military are likely to intervene, promising order, or a **charismatic** leader is likely to gather support by promising a better future.

29

How dictatorships are justified

No dictatorship – personal or collective – openly admits to holding power for the benefit of the rulers rather than the ruled. Common justifications for dictatorship include:

- Restoring order in a country torn by riots and strikes, for example General Primo de Rivera in Spain in 1923 or General Pinochet in Chile in 1973. Primo de Rivera lost the support of the army and fell from power in 1930, opening the way to further disorder and then civil war from 1936 to 1939. Pinochet allowed Chile to return to democracy in 1989.
- The alleged breakdown of a constitution, for example the military take-over in Burma in 1962. They have ruled Burma ever since, refusing to recognize the results of an election held in 1990, in which a civilian, democratic party won a two-thirds majority.
- The incompetence or oppression of a leader, for example the overthrow in 1966 of Ahmed Sukarno, Indonesia's independence leader, by General Suharto. Suharto's hugely corrupt regime was even worse, wasting Indonesia's natural riches on a massive scale until popular unrest forced him to resign in 1998.
- Defending a successful revolution, for example the permanent rule of the Institutional Revolutionary Party (PRI) in Mexico from the 1920s until 1997.
- Ending foreign business influence over the economy, for example the rule of Colonel Juan Péron in Argentina in the 1950s. Péron was driven into exile but returned for a second, unsuccessful term of office as elected president in 1973–74.
- Cleaning up financial corruption, for example numerous military take-overs in Nigeria. In Ghana Flight Lieutenant Jerry Rawlings seized power for this purpose in 1979 and 1981 and actually did make government more honest. He was re-elected President in free elections in 1992 and 1996.
- Ending alleged political corruption, for example General Zia ul-Haq's overthrow of the civilian government of Zulfikar Ali Bhutto in Pakistan in 1977. Zia ruled until his death in an air crash in 1988. Bhutto's daughter, Benazir, was twice elected prime minister until she, too, was disgraced by corruption, though this time it was financial, rather than political. The military, led by General Pervez Musharaff, seized power again in 1999.
- The promise of a better tomorrow for every citizen in return for discipline, effort and sacrifice now. This is the most widely used justification of all, and was employed by most communist regimes, states such as Syria under Hafez al-Assad (1930–2000), as well as Iraq under Saddam Hussein (1937–) or Ghana under Kwame Nkrumah. These states claim to be building a socialist society of welfare for all.

⑤ Fascism and its friends

Mussolini's Italy

Italy was on the winning side in World War I but gained little from it in return for huge losses and expense. Thousands of ex-soldiers felt betrayed and resentful. A newly-founded **communist** party called for revolution. Benito Mussolini (1883–1945), a war veteran and journalist, recruited *Fasci di Combattimenti* (bands of fighters) to fight the communists. Mussolini claimed to know how history was unfolding and promised that under his guidance Italy would move forward to a glorious future.

A march-past of the Italian fascist youth movement, wearing the party's black-shirt uniform. Students, like the unemployed and many ex-servicemen, found that the fascist movement offered them comradeship and a sense of purpose lacking in **civilian** life.

The years after World War I saw violent **demonstrations**, organized street-fighting between **fascists** and communists and the disruption of daily life by repeated strikes. The fear of revolution created a situation in which many longed for the restoration of order, even at the cost of normal political freedoms.

Mussolini claimed to have seized power by force as a result of a March on Rome in 1922, but this was a myth that suited his image as a strong man. In fact, he became prime minister of Italy quite legally, at the invitation of King Victor Emmanuel III. Mussolini's dictatorship was achieved over several years. Gradually the fascist party gained full power over politics and the media, replacing parliament with a Chamber of Corporations. This was supposed to represent groups such as labour, farmers and intellectuals, and by doing so to have overcome traditional conflicts between employers and workers in the interest of the nation as a whole. Fascist posters proclaimed *Mussolini ha sempre ragione* (Mussolini is always right) and projected images of Il Duce (the leader) as a 20th-century Caesar who would restore the ancient glories of the mighty Roman empire. Mussolini's power was limited by the strength of the Catholic church, which he was careful not to attack. Mussolini also sidelined the Italian **monarchy** rather than abolishing it. Once he had achieved power, Mussolini used little violence to maintain his position. Four thousand anti-fascists were imprisoned and thousands more beaten up, but only ten were actually killed.

Mussolini poses for a bust of himself as a grim-faced hero.

Image of a leader

Both Mussolini and Hitler styled themselves 'Leader' and took immense trouble over the image that the mass media projected of them. But the style that each chose was very different.

Hitler was usually portrayed as serious, aloof and distant, almost as a divine figure, staring into a future that only he had the wisdom to foresee. Mussolini, by contrast, played a variety of roles, from warrior, decked out in military uniform, to man of culture, playing the violin, to family man, surrounded by his children. He was even photographed, stripped to the waist, helping peasants to gather the harvest. For Hitler this would have been unimaginable. The Italian press was told that Mussolini's name was always to be printed in capital letters and they were never to print pictures that might contradict his strong man image, such as showing him dancing or talking to a priest.

Stalin, who ordered or organized the deaths of millions, was frequently portrayed as a kindly father figure, surrounded by crowds of adoring small children, offering him bouquets of flowers. During the war his image incorporated traditional Russian **patriotism**, such as the shadows of past heroes in the background.

Mussolini's attempts to modernize Italy's economy did strengthen industries with military importance, such as the metal and chemical industries. Roads and railways were improved for the same reason. Electricity output tripled between 1920 and 1935. Strikes were banned, along with beauty contests and the reporting of crime. Population growth was encouraged so that Italy could have a bigger army. As a result, bachelors were taxed for being single, women were banned from government jobs and everyone employed by the government, from teachers to postmen, was ordered to marry or lose their job.

To re-establish Italy as a great imperial power, Mussolini devoted a quarter of all government spending to the armed forces, conquering Ethiopia and sending 50,000 troops to fight for Franco in the Spanish Civil War. These adventures were a terrible waste of resources. When Mussolini disastrously decided to join in World War II, Italy simply could not arm its soldiers and its forces found themselves fighting with tanks, planes and ships far inferior to their opponents. There were disastrous defeats in the Balkans and North Africa. This created an anti-war group among the military, which overthrew Mussolini in 1943.

As the monarchy still survived, it provided an alternative focus for national loyalty. Italian **partisans** fought on the Allied side against an occupying German army which killed 36,000 of them and shot 10,000 more in **reprisals**. Mussolini was rescued from imprisonment by **Nazi** special forces and set up a powerless puppet-state, the Republic of Salo, with Nazi backing. Nazi defeat made him flee in disguise. He was caught by communist partisans and shot. The war cost Italy a third of its national wealth and 300,000 dead.

Nazi Germany

Hitler, too, came to power in 1933 by legal means, at the invitation of the President of Germany's **republican** government and as leader of the largest single party in the Reichstag (German parliament). He was supported by experienced political and business leaders who aimed to control him for their own ends. Hitler aimed to crush communism and put a powerful Germany at the head of a reorganized Europe. This would be free from Jews, **Slavs** and other *Untermenschen* (sub-humans), who would be reduced to slavery and eventually wiped out.

Within a month of Hitler's coming to power, the Reichstag burned down. Just how and why was not clear, but it gave Hitler a golden chance to declare a state of emergency and get the members of the Reichstag to grant him powers to rule by **decree**. The Reichstag itself was soon abolished. Members of the Nazi secret service and armed **militias** were given police powers. A campaign of *Gleichschaltung* (streamlining) removed from the armed forces, law courts, civil service, education system, big business and media everyone the Nazis regarded as enemies – Jews, communists, **socialists** and many leaders of trade unions and churches. Hundreds of thousands of writers, teachers, lawyers, scientists and artists fled abroad. Hundreds of thousands more were arrested and sent to concentration camps, along with gypsies, homosexuals and beggars. In theory they were there to be re-educated through work and lectures. In practice they were starved, beaten, tortured or executed.

A Nazi election poster claims that a vote for Hitler will free Germany from the chains of despair and humiliation. Hitler's appeal to the German electorate was his promise to restore the nation's shattered pride and put unemployed millions back to work – which he did with speedy success.

35

The Nazi take-over of Germany was far more rapid and far more complete than the fascist take-over in Italy. It was also far more bloody. There was no monarchy as an alternative focus of loyalty. Divided between Protestant and Catholic, the churches were also much weaker in their opposition. As Germany was much richer and more technologically advanced than Italy, Nazi dictatorship could be much more efficient. Mass-produced radios were installed in every school, railway station and public building, so that Hitler could address the entire nation whenever he wanted.

Hitler, unlike Mussolini, did equip his armed forces well. He put Germans back to work, built impressive apartment blocks and *Autobahnen* (motorways) and hosted the 1936 Olympics in Berlin to show off the superiority of the Germans as the world 'Master Race'. Unemployment fell from six million in 1933 to 300,000 by 1939. Nazi supporters were rewarded with homes, businesses, art treasures and belongings stolen from Jews driven into flight. Workers lost the right to free trade unions but got cheap holidays.

Hitler's aims were summed up in a series of simple slogans. The overriding idea was that the Germans were the world's greatest people. Purged of foreign influences (especially Jewish), and united by a disciplined movement, the nation would march forward to dominate the world. The idea that Germans should be '*Ein Reich, Ein Volk, Ein Führer*' (one state, one people, one leader) led Hitler to demand that Germany's borders should expand to take in all *Auslandsdeutsche* – Germans living under foreign rule. This led to a Nazi take-over of Austria, the border areas of Czechoslovakia and the port of Memel in Lithuania. Applying this aim to Poland started World War II in September 1939.

Crowds and power

Mass-meetings and rallies have been an important feature of dictatorial **regimes**. They provide a substitute for reasoned argument and an opportunity to play on emotions. Both Hitler and Mussolini were brilliant public speakers, able to whip huge crowds into a frenzy of hatred or adoration. Major rallies were carefully stage-managed and often held at night, so that flaming torches or blazing searchlights could be used to dramatic effect, concentrating all attention on the leader and drowning distractions in darkness. Every September, Nazis from all over Germany gathered at Nuremberg for a huge rally. In 1936 Hitler told them, 'Not every one of you sees me and I do not see every one of you. But I feel you and you feel me.... we are with him and he with us, and we are now Germany !'

Hitler explained the power of the mass meeting in his book, *Mein Kampf* (*My Struggle*), 'in it the individual, who at first ... feels lonely ... gets the picture of a larger community which in most people has a strengthening, encouraging effect ... the visible ... agreement of thousands confirms to him the rightness of his new belief ... The will, the longing and also the power of thousands are concentrated in every individual.'

Hitler arrives at the Berlin Olympic Stadium to address a crowd of 132,000 members of the Hitler Youth organization.

Poland was defeated within weeks. The following spring German armies defeated and occupied Belgium, the Netherlands, Denmark, Norway and France. In summer they smashed hundreds of miles into the **Soviet Union**. Disastrous German defeats began in 1942, but it took three more years to destroy the Nazi regime. Whereas few Italians were prepared to die for fascism and many were glad to fight against it, the hold of the Nazi dictatorship over the German people proved much harder to break. The defeat of Nazism cost Germany three-and-a-half million dead, 12 million refugees and the division of the country into two separate states for half a century. Both Fascist Italy and Nazi Germany promised prosperity, but by aggression in war brought defeat which destroyed their achievements.

Imitators and allies

The inter-war regimes of Hungary under Admiral Horthy (1868–1957), Poland under General Pilsudski (1867–1935), Austria under Chancellor Dollfuss (1892–1934) and Portugal under Antonio Salazar (1889–1970) are better described as **authoritarian** than completely dictatorial. All were fiercely anti–communist, but they permitted a limited degree of political freedom for some parties and newspapers and respected the influence of the Roman Catholic church. General Franco (1892–1975), commander of the military rebels who had destroyed the Spanish republic in a terrible civil war (1936–39), refused to be drawn into World War II and, free from outside interference, made good his hold on power. He ruled until his death in 1975 but arranged for the monarchy to be restored under King Juan Carlos I, who swiftly returned Spain to democracy.

During World War II, the Nazis installed fascist figureheads in short-lived puppet-states they created in Slovakia and Croatia. In Romania General Antonescu (1882–1946) drove King Carol into exile, proclaimed himself the nation's *Conducator* (guide) and plunged it into a catastrophic alliance with Germany against the USSR.

⑥ What dictatorships achieve

The impact of **dictatorship** varies greatly according to the personality and aims of the dictator and the circumstances he faces. The following examples show a range of possibilities. The first group of dictators can perhaps claim to have had good intentions for their people, the second were simply out for themselves. These examples also show that there is no simple link between a ruler's intentions and their results, or between a country's natural wealth and its people's prosperity.

Remaking nations

This first group of dictators set out with the aim of remodelling and modernizing their countries to bring greater prosperity to their people.

Atatürk

What is now the **republic** of Turkey was once the core of the sprawling, multi-ethnic Ottoman Empire. Over six centuries it had spread from its homeland on the Anatolian plateau northwards into the Balkans and southwards into Arabia. Ruled by a sultan who claimed to be the heir (khalifa, or caliph) of the prophet Muhammad, the empire was based on Islam, but tolerated Christians and Jews.

During the 19th century, sultans tried to update their armed forces using mainly German advisers, and the sultan sided with Germany in World War I. Defeat cost the Ottomans most of their territories outside Anatolia and tempted Greece to take more by war. The Greeks were soundly beaten by the Turkish general Mustafa Kemal. Hailed as a hero, Kemal accepted the loss of non-Turkish territories, abolished the Caliphate and made Turkey a republic with himself as president.

Blaming defeat in World War I on the backwardness, corruption and incompetence of Ottoman rule, Kemal aimed to remodel the new Turkey on modern, western lines. This not only meant boosting industry, education and transport but changing traditional customs to fit in with European standards, such as abandoning the Islamic calendar and Arabic script. Kemal threw himself completely into his mission, leading by example under the slogan 'Be proud you are Turkish'.

Because Turks revered Kemal as a complete **patriot**, head and shoulders above all other leaders, they accepted such dramatic changes as votes for women and moving the capital to Ankara in the heart of Anatolia. All Turks were required to take western-style family names and Kemal became known as Atatürk – Father of the Turks. Islam was too powerful for Atatürk to abolish, but he aimed to keep it out of politics by banning many Islamic organizations and making education purely **secular**. Atatürk's long-term intention was to turn Turkey into a genuine **democracy** with competing political parties, but in his own lifetime he tolerated little opposition to his reforms.

Mustafa Kemal Atatürk (1881–1938) (left) was like a dictator in the Roman sense, rescuing his country from crisis. He set an example of wearing western dress to show Turks what it meant to be a modern people.

The depth of national mourning at his death showed that Atatürk was genuinely respected for his achievements. His picture still adorns every school, post office, town hall and public building in Turkey. Islam, however, has re-emerged as a force in Turkish politics and the Turkish armed forces have intervened in politics periodically as the self-appointed guardians of Kemalism.

The Pahlavi dynasty

Atatürk's example was followed in Iran by Reza Khan (1878–1944) an army officer who overthrew the last shah of the Kajar dynasty, declaring himself shah of a new Pahlavi dynasty. His efforts to westernize Iran were much less successful, partly because he lacked Atatürk's popular support, partly because the hold of Islam on everyday life was even stronger than in Turkey. His son, Mohammad Reza Shah Pahlavi (1919–80), pushed westernization even harder, provoking a backlash which led to his overthrow and the establishment of an Islamic republic in 1979.

Nkrumah

Kwame Nkrumah (1909–72) led the British West African **colony** of Gold Coast to independence in 1957 by largely peaceful means and became its first president. Nkrumah changed the country's name to Ghana, the name of a past great African empire. This was a clue to Nkrumah's long-term aim of bringing together former European colonies in Africa into a new united Africa, under the leadership of Ghana and himself. Nkrumah had spent many years abroad, studying in Britain and the USA. He promoted himself as a great thinker and published many books on political questions and the nature of African culture. Many of these were probably written by other people.

41

Nkrumah (waving) chose to wear the robes of a chief to show respect for African tradition and independence from the West.

Ghana itself was, by African standards, well-off at independence, thanks to its thriving cocoa industry. Nkrumah used government revenue to put up impressive buildings, create new industries and support prestige projects like a national airline. In reality, these ventures were not what Ghana needed and they wasted resources that could have been better spent on improving such services as rural roads and basic healthcare. But Nkrumah was in a hurry to show results and ignored the fact that most government-supported businesses were inefficient and corrupt. At the same time he devoted much of his time and energy to foreign travel and meetings because he was determined to show himself as a major international statesman. In the end, his efforts to create pan-African unity led to nothing.

Meanwhile Nkrumah's methods of governing became increasingly dictatorial, as he blamed political opponents for his failure to turn Ghana into a major industrial power overnight. As early as 1958, he introduced a law allowing for suspected enemies to be arrested and imprisoned without trial and without any specific charge being made against them. The media was strictly censored to publish only stories that made Nkrumah and Ghana look successful. Trade unions, universities and the law courts were brought under strict government control. In 1964 Nkrumah decreed that there would be only one political party which he would lead. He declared that he would be president for the rest of his life.

In 1966, while Nkrumah was away in Beijing, the Ghanaian military seized power. Nkrumah's close friend, Sékou Touré, dictatorial president of Guinea, gave him a home. In 1972 Nkrumah died of cancer in hospital in Romania, where he had been offered treatment by the country's **communist** dictator, Nicolae Ceausescu. Ghana was left to struggle out of the mess into which he had led it. Nkrumah's magnificent presidential palace is now a forgotten ruin.

Castro

Cuba won its independence from Spain in 1902, but the USA came to dominate its economy and often interfered in its politics to protect American business interests. Fulgencio Batista was dictator of Cuba from 1952 to 1959. By this time, a few Cubans were very wealthy and most were very poor. Despite its large army, Batista's regime was overthrown by Cuban exile Fidel Castro (1927–) whose **guerrilla** force of a few dozen men turned into a tidal wave of discontent. Batista's soldiers and police simply crumbled before it.

Castro's **regime** confiscated much wealth, including many US-owned businesses. This led to US trade **sanctions** which turned Castro towards the USSR as an alternative source of trade, aid and weapons. Castro announced his

conversion to communism and the **Soviet Union's** support
became the mainstay of the economy. Cuba's prosperity depended
almost entirely on sugar, rum and cigars, which were exported to
the USSR and its allies. In return, Cuba sent troops to fight for
pro-Soviet movements in countries such as Angola.

Castro's regime stressed building up health and education for all.
As a result Cubans have the highest life expectancy in Latin
America (76 years) and a **literacy** rate of 96 per cent, outranking
neighbouring Jamaica (86 per cent) and resource-rich Brazil
(84 per cent). Sport was also given a high priority as a way of
winning international prestige.

The Cuban Anier Garcia (centre) takes gold in the 110-metre hurdles
at the 2000 Sydney Olympics. Cuban athletes, especially sprinters and
boxers, have performed outstandingly at international level.

On the other hand, hundreds of thousands of Cubans hated Castro's
rule so much that they risked death by drowning in dangerous and
shark-infested seas to flee abroad in small boats.

The collapse of the USSR greatly damaged the Cuban economy, forcing it to build up tourism as an alternative source of income. Castro remains in power, but what will happen after his death is uncertain.

Plundering nations

Political scientists have invented the term 'kleptocracy' – rule by thieves – to describe the style of dictatorial government which loots a country of its wealth for the personal benefit of the ruler, his family and henchmen. Africa, rich in resources but weak in its institutions and starved of skilled political manpower to build them, has provided dramatic examples.

Bokassa

Jean-Bédel Bokassa (1921–96) won numerous bravery awards in the French colonial army before rising rapidly to become chief of staff of the newly independent Central African Republic. He seized power in a coup in 1966. Bokassa not only had opponents killed but personally took part in the murder of 100 schoolchildren.

'Emperor' Bokassa's coronation. After declaring himself president for life, in 1977 Bokassa spent $20,000,000 – a third of his government's annual revenue – on having himself crowned emperor, in imitation of his hero, Napoleon.

45

For trade reasons, successive French governments supported Bokassa until an embarrassing scandal broke over a diamond given to French President Giscard d'Estaing. After Bokassa physically attacked the French ambassador, French paratroopers overthrew him by force, while pretending that the coup was an internal affair. Bokassa fled to exile, but returned voluntarily in 1986 to serve seven years for the murder of schoolchildren.

Amin

Idi Amin (1925–), though barely literate, became a senior officer of the Ugandan army under President Milton Obote (1924–), who relied on him to suppress opposition. Then, fearing Amin's power, Obote was about to replace him when Amin struck first. Amin initially gave the world's media the impression of being a rather simple-minded, slightly ridiculous soldier, but he soon resorted to rule by pure terror.

In 1972 the entire Asian business community was expelled, so that the new regime could plunder their property. The Asians were relatively fortunate in at least getting away with their lives, as an estimated 300,000 Ugandans died under Amin's rule (1971–79). Amin personally murdered dozens of people, including the Anglican archbishop, feeding many of his victims to crocodiles.

The economy fell apart in chaos and, despite the help of Libyan troops, Amin's forces collapsed before an invading army of Ugandan exiles, supported by the regular army of neighbouring Tanzania. Amin fled to safety in Libya and then Saudi Arabia, where he still lives.

Mobutu

Congo, fabulously rich with gold, diamonds, copper, cobalt, oil and timber, was misruled from 1965 to 1997 by ex-soldier-turned-journalist President Mobutu (1930–97). He was a former general who changed the country's name to Zaire as part of his programme to return the country to what he claimed was a genuinely African culture. For the same reason he changed his own name from Joseph-Désiré Mobutu to Mobutu Sese Seko Kuku Ngbendu Wa Za Banga ('the all-powerful warrior who, because of his endurance and inflexible will to win, will go from conquest to conquest, leaving fire in his wake').

Mobutu shared the vanity of Bokassa and Amin, but without their taste for murder. The damage he inflicted was caused more by corruption, neglect and massive incompetence than by systematic cruelty. Protected by a bodyguard recruited from his own Ngbandi people, Mobutu played on the rivalries of Congo's 250 other ethnic groups to provide excuses for the failures of his rule. By posing as a strong anti-communist, he also gained aid and military support from the USA, France, Belgium and Israel – but also accepted military advisers from communist China and North Korea.

By the 1980s Mobutu's personal fortune was estimated at $4 billion, not to mention his 20 overseas properties, valued at $37 million. Anti-communism ceased to protect Mobutu with the ending of the Cold War (1990) and during the 1990s he was on the defensive. In 1997 he was driven out by his own failing health and a rebel movement supported by democratic South Africa, the USA and most of Zaire's neighbours. He died in **exile**.

Banda

The rule of ex-doctor Hastings Banda (1898–1997) in Malawi was far less bloody and chaotic than the three previous examples, though Banda did have political opponents gaoled and executed. Scornful of the opinion of other black African leaders, Banda was happy to trade with South Africa and accept aid from its government, even though it oppressed its own black population. Living standards in Malawi rose slowly but steadily as Banda promoted himself from prime minister (1963) to president for life (1971). Banda's own living standards certainly rose, until senility forced him out. His death revealed that he had exported some $320 million to overseas bank accounts.

Ceausescu

The nearest the communist world has come to a kleptocracy is
Romania under the rule of Nicolae Ceausescu (1918–89).
Ceausescu joined the illegal communist party as a teenager and
was imprisoned for this in 1936–38 and 1940–44. A member of
the party's central committee at 27, he took 20 years to become
general secretary but then concentrated power in his own hands
to become commander-in-chief and head of state as well.

Ceausescu appointed family members to positions of power which
they used to enrich themselves. Meanwhile, to pay off Romania's
foreign debts he forced it to export food and oil, causing acute
shortages of both at home. In 1983 even TV was rationed to two
hours a day, most of it about Ceausescu and his wife, Elena, who
were shown as brilliant leaders, adored everywhere they went.
Ceausescu's plans to make Romania a powerful modern country
included ordering every family to have at least five children.
Dozens of traditional villages were bulldozed to force people to live
in apartment blocks, where they could be more easily controlled.
Meanwhile, the Ceausescus and their family lived in luxurious
palaces. Opposition was crushed by a 100,000-strong police force,
the Securitate.

On 17 December 1989, demonstrators protested in the provincial
city of Timisoara. Hundreds were shot, provoking further protests in
the capital Bucharest, on the 21st. When the army sided with the
protesters against the Securitate the rule of the Ceausescus ended
with their flight, capture and immediate trial for 'crimes against the
people', including the deaths of over 60,000. They were shot on
Christmas Day 1989.

These five examples constitute a mixed record. Bokassa left a poor
country poorer still. Amin, Mobutu and Ceausescu reduced
resource-rich countries to poverty and disorder. Banda did provide
stability and a measure of prosperity, though his missing millions
could have been used to benefit his people.

⑦ How dictatorships end

Searching for stability

Atatürk's Turkey and Mexico after the revolution of 1910–20 did grow into **democracies**. In 20th-century Spain, Greece, Chile, Argentina and Brazil, democracy has been successfully restored after periods of dictatorial or military rule. In Nigeria, Pakistan, Thailand and Peru, the military have repeatedly intervened in politics, leading to periods of strong-man rule by generals. However, their armed forces have also repeatedly shown a willingness to go back to their barracks and turn the problems of running the country back to **civilian** politicians.

Communist collapses

The break-up of the **Soviet Union** in 1990–91 enabled the populations of its former allies in eastern Europe to overthrow their own **communist** governments through mass demonstrations. Poland was already well on the way to democracy thanks to its Solidarity movement, based on its trade-unions. In East Germany and Czechoslovakia, the changeover was almost bloodless, in Romania it was violent. The ending of the Cold War has made the USA much less willing to maintain links with dictatorial governments simply because they claim to be strongly anti-communist. This, and increasing public anger in western democracies at human rights abuses, has made it harder for **dictatorships** to benefit from trade and contacts with democratic countries and the global corporations based in them. One result of this has been the general disappearance of dictatorships in Latin America since the 1980s.

Death and disorder

As in the world of ancient Greece, the simple fact of the death of the dictator can be enough to end his **regime**, though this can be the prelude to chaos rather than freedom and stability.

Yugoslavia's wartime guerrilla leader Marshal Tito (1892–1980) managed to create a communist state which was fiercely independent of the USSR. He also controlled the tensions between the country's different nationalities. Tito left behind a leadership team which maintained this stability for a decade, until old rivalries between Serbs, Croats and Bosnians led to disastrous wars of partition and the emergence of **authoritarian** regimes under Slobodan Milosevic in Serbia and Franjo Tudjman in Croatia. In neighbouring Albania, the death of Enver Hoxha in 1985 brought to an end 40 years of communist dictatorship which left the country the poorest in Europe and led to a decline into general criminality which threatens the stability of its Balkan neighbours.

Family ties

Perhaps remarkably, family loyalties can still prove as important in some 20th century states as they were in medieval kingdoms, where sons followed fathers onto the throne.

In regimes dominated by a single leader, a funeral offers the opportunity to show loyalty. Here Bashar al-Assad (facing camera with raised fist, left), successor and son of Hafez al-Assad as ruler of Syria accompanies his father's coffin.

On the wretchedly poor Caribbean island of Haiti, François 'Papa Doc' Duvalier ruled from 1957 to 1971 by a mixture of corruption and terror. He gained support from the rural black poor against the traditionally powerful mulatto (mixed race) élite of the towns. He even managed to pass on his position to his teenage son, Jean-Claude 'Baby Doc' Duvalier, who was not overthrown until 1986. Despite US attempts to stabilize Haiti, by using troops to guarantee order and by supervising fair elections, Haiti has remained prone to political violence.

North Korea is the only remaining state to cling to the hard-line communism of Stalin's day. The dictator Kim Il-Sung (know as the 'Great Leader'), ruled from 1948 to 1994 and managed to pass his position on to his son Kim Jong-Il (known as the 'Dear Leader'), who has ruled ever since, despite the fact that the country's massive spending on armaments has impoverished it and brought widespread famine.

The cult of personality

Concentrating power in the hands of a single individual has led to the emergence of a cult of personality in both **fascist** and communist regimes. Concentrating loyalty on a personality not only increased their power, but distracted attention from gaps or contradictions in their political programme. So long as the leader wields power everything is, by definition, under control. At its most extreme, the cult of personality presents the leader as a universal genius, worthy not just of obedience but of adoration and the highest sacrifice. Members of the Hitler Youth were required to swear, 'to devote all my energies and my strength to the saviour of our country, Adolf Hitler. I am willing and ready to give up my life for him, so help me God.' Although Stalin himself was largely responsible for the disastrous defeats suffered by the Soviet army at the hands of German invaders, Soviet propaganda hailed him as a military genius.

Perhaps the most extreme personality cult was built up around the North Korean communist leader, Kim Il Sung (1912–94) and his son and successor Kim Jong-Il (1941–) who is referred to by the media as, 'The peerless commander, heaven on earth and saviour of the Korean people.' In February 2002 Kim Jong-Il's sixtieth birthday was marked by an inscription in his honour carved onto a mountainside in letters 34 metres high.

Isolation

Officially Libya has a People's Government, which claims to have abolished its institutions, such as its police force and law courts and replaced them with committees of ordinary citizens. In practice, the country is controlled by Colonel Muammar al-Qaddafi, who has ruled since he overthrew the monarchy in 1969. Like Nkrumah, Qaddafi has presented himself as a great thinker. The *Green Book* he wrote sets out his 'Third Universal Theory' which claims to be the key to solving all political and economic problems. Like Nkrumah, Qaddafi has tried to put himself at the head of a unity movement, in his case pan-Arab. He has supported terrorists in neighbouring countries such as Egypt, Sudan and Chad, as well as in Northern Ireland, supplying weapons, money, training and a safe refuge. Although Qaddafi has had opponents killed at home and abroad he aims to present himself as a simple Muslim with no personal taste for power or wealth. United Nations **sanctions** on travel and trade with Libya have kept the country isolated, but Qaddafi's government has been able to survive thanks to its oil, which makes it relatively wealthy in relation to its small population.

There is no pretence at democracy in the Iraq of Saddam Hussein. Effective dictator of Iraq since 1979, he used the country's oil wealth to bring jobs, welfare and electricity to the poor, giving many people good reasons to be grateful for his rule. A long (1980–88) war against neighbouring Iran cost hundreds of thousands of lives and brought no gains, but failed to shake his position. Nor did his invasion of neighbouring Kuwait. Iraqi forces were thrown out of Kuwait by a US-led coalition in 1991 at the cost of another 100,000 lives. Despite UN sanctions isolating Iraq ever since, Saddam Hussein remains in power. Surrounded by family members and henchmen from his home town of Takrit, he takes elaborate precautions against assassination and has himself personally murdered his opponents.

Huge paintings of Saddam Hussein dominate public places in Iraq. Dictators typically devote large resources to maintaining their popularity and belief in their right to rule by means of propaganda through rallies, demonstrations, posters, newspapers, films and school textbooks.

In 1975 Pol Pot (1925–98), a founder of the local communist party, seized power in Cambodia with the backing of a **guerrilla** army of peasants, known as the Khmer Rouge. The country had been badly affected by the spill-over effects of war in neighbouring Vietnam, which had killed 150,000 Cambodians and made 2,000,000 homeless. Pol Pot's answer was to cut all contacts with the outside world and make Cambodia self-supporting by forcing city dwellers to work on the land.

53

His Khmer Rouge government banned money, religion, foreign languages, newspapers, radio, TV and even bicycles. Two million people, a quarter of the entire population, were killed or died of starvation before Pol Pot was overthrown by a Vietnamese invasion in 1979. Pol Pot led Khmer Rouge guerilla resistance to Cambodia's new Vietnamese-backed government for another seventeen years. He finally lost control of the Khmer Rouge and was arrested by them, but died naturally before he could be tried for his crimes.

Can dictatorships survive?

Dictatorship may be in decline, but it is by no means dead. Remarkably, presidents Assad in Syria and Kim in North Korea managed to pass on their positions to their sons, like tyrants in the ancient Greek world. It remains to be seen how long they can hang on to power. Both Saddam and Qaddafi may also attempt to prepare the way for a successor from within their own family. A vicious struggle for power is quite as likely, whatever they attempt or intend. Terror as a tool of political power is under attack internationally. In the long run, the ever freer movement of people and ideas will combat its use within states as well as between them. Dictatorship, as the ancient Greeks came to understand, is basically an unstable form of government and cannot endure.

So, what is dictatorship?

Dictatorship was known to the ancient Greeks, but only became prominent as a form of government after Napoleon. Modern dictatorship is distinguished by its ruthless use of force and its concern to mobilize active support for its efforts to change society. The existence of strong alternative institutions, such as a **monarchy**, army or church, has tended to limit the changes a dictatorship can bring about. When a dictatorship succeeds in neutralizing or destroying such institutions, its potential for the abuse of power is greatly increased.

The most extreme dictatorships have brought disaster on their countries. Adolf Hitler aimed to rid the world of **communism** but instead ensured that half of Europe, including half of Germany itself would be ruled by communists for half a century. The 1959 census figures for the USSR make it possible to calculate that, thanks to Stalin's persecutions in the 1930s, its population was 20% smaller than it would otherwise have been. In 1958 Mao Zedong called on China to make a Great Leap Forward and create modern industries overnight. The result was failed harvests and mass-starvation. In 1966 he launched a Cultural Revolution to restore his personal leadership of the party. Led by fanatical young Red Guards, mobs attacked figures in authority such as party officials, factory managers and teachers. About half a million people were killed and the country's education system and industry were set back years.

The rapid destruction of the cruel Taliban regime in Afghanistan in 2001 shows that dictatorship's own weapons can be turned against it. In the same year, the former dictator of Serbia, Slobodan Milosevic, was brought before an international tribunal for crimes against the peoples of the Balkans. This shows an emerging belief in the world community that such abuses of power must be brought to account.

Timeline

138–78 BC	Sulla, Roman dictator
c.102–44 BC	Julius Caesar, Roman dictator
1513	Niccolo Machiavelli of Florence publishes *The Prince*, a handbook for ruthless rulers
1653–58	Oliver Cromwell rules Britain as Lord Protector
1804–15	Napoleon rules France as emperor
1819–25	Simon Bolivar liberates former Spanish colonies of South America
1852–70	Napoleon III rules a Second Empire in France
1914–18	World War I
1917	Communist revolution overthrows royal rule in Russia
1922	Mussolini's March on Rome
1923	General Primo de Rivera seizes power in Spain General Mustafa Kemal declares Turkey a republic
1928	Stalin becomes unopposed ruler of the Soviet Union
1933	Hitler comes to power in Germany
1936–39	Francisco Franco wins civil war in Spain to become *Caudillo*
1945	Fascist regime overthrown in Germany
1949	George Orwell publishes *Nineteen eighty-four*
1959	Fidel Castro overthrows Fulgencio Batista in Cuba
1962	Military takeover in Burma
1966	General Suharto overthrows Ahmed Sukarno in Indonesia Kwame Nkrumah overthrown by a military coup in Ghana
1969	Colonel Muammar Qaddafi overthrows the monarchy in Libya
1973	General Pinochet seizes power in Chile
1975	Spain restored to democracy by King Juan Carlos I
1977	General Zia ul-Haq overthrows civilian rule of Zulfikar Ali Bhutto in Pakistan Jean-Bedel Bokassa of the Central African Republic crowns himself Emperor

1979	Ayatollah Ruhollah Khomeini leads an Islamic Revolution in Iran
	Idi Amin flees from Uganda
	Saddam Hussein becomes undisputed dictator of Iraq
1985	Collapse of communist dictatorship in Albania with death of Enver Hoxha
1986	'Baby Doc' Duvalier overthrown in Haiti
1989–91	Break-up of the Soviet Union
1991	Overthrow of Colonel Mengistu in Ethiopia
1999	General Pervez Musharraf takes power in Pakistan
2001	Slobodan Milosevic charged with war crimes and crimes against humanity at an international tribunal in The Hague
2002	Saddam Hussein's 65th birthday is celebrated throughout Iraq despite his poor record on human rights

⑨ Further reading

Nigel Kelly, *Russia and the USSR 1905–1956* (History Through Sources, Heinemann Library, 1997)

George Orwell, *Nineteen Eighty-four* (Penguin, 2000)

Terry Pratchett, *Small Gods* (Gollancz, 1992)

Fiona Reynoldson, *Weimar and Nazi Germany* (History Through Sources, Heinemann Library, 1997)

Richard Tames, *Fascism* (Hodder, 2000)

David Taylor, *Adolf Hitler* (Leading Lives, Heinemann Library, 2001)

Sources

Paul Brooker, *Twentieth Century Dictatorships* (Macmillan, 1995)

Paul Brooker, *Non-Democratic Regimes: Theory, Government and Politics* (Macmillan Press, 2000)

Clive Carpenter, *The Guinness Book of Kings, Rulers and Statesmen* (Guinness, 1978)

J. Denis Derbyshire and Ian Derbyshire, *Spotlight on World Political Systems: An Introduction to Comparative Government* (Chambers, 1991)

J. Denis Derbyshire and Ian Derbyshire, *Political Systems of the World* (W. & R. Chambers, 1996)

Dennis Kavanagh, *Dictionary of Political Biography* (Oxford University Press, 1998)

Barry Rubin, *Modern Dictators: A History of Tyranny in the Third World* (W.H. Allen, 1987)

Websites

There is a light-hearted website at: www.thedictatorship.com

BBC: www.bbc.co.uk/

Guardian Unlimited: www.guardian.co.uk

The Electronic Telegraph: www.telegraph.co.uk

CIA: www.cia.gov/

Library of Congress: www.loc.gov/

Washington Post: www.washpostco.com

Some 20th-century dictators

Mao Zedong (1893–1976) Founder of Communist China Born a farmer's son, Mao became active in student politics, founding the Chinese Communist Party in 1921. Mao adapted **communist** theory to suit the needs of Chinese peasants, setting up a peasant-led commune at Jiangxi in 1931–34. When Chinese Nationalists attacked it, he led 100,000 followers on a 9700-kilometre (6000-mile) Long March (1934–36) to the safety of Yenan. Two-thirds of the marchers died but from there Mao led **guerrilla** resistance to Japanese invasion and later defeated the Nationalists, declaring China an independent communist state in 1949. Mao ordered the disastrous Great Leap Forward (1958–60) and the hugely destructive Cultural Revolution (1966–69). He was an accomplished poet, and his political writings were regarded as works of genius by the fanatical young Red Guards who did his bidding. Despite his responsibility for up to 20,000,000 deaths, Mao is still honoured for ending years of foreign interference in China.

Juan Péron (1895–1974) Dictator of Argentina 1946–55 Handsome, charming, a champion skier and fencer, Péron was a professional army officer who had lived in and admired Mussolini's Italy. As one of the military who seized power in Argentina in 1943, Péron built up a personal following among trade unions there, which enabled him to become president in 1946. He was a brilliant public speaker but gained even more popularity through his glamorous wife, Evita (1919–52), a minor actress with a genius for publicizing her charity work. Péron's attacks on foreign-owned businesses were as popular as his welfare reforms and support for local industry. Péron and Evita were genuinely adored by the poor and her sudden early death from cancer plunged the nation into grief. Péron then lost his touch with the people, angered the powerful Catholic church and army, brought the economy to ruin and was driven into exile. Support for Péronism survived, however, and in 1973 Péron returned in triumph. However, he failed to solve Argentina's continuing problems, and died after a year. His third wife, Isabelita (1931–), took over but was overthrown by the army in 1976.

Augusto Pinochet (1915–) Dictator of Chile 1973–90 A professional army officer, Pinochet led the military to overthrow the legally elected government of Salvador Allende, whose reforms for the poor were held to damage business. Pinochet's government imprisoned, tortured and murdered opponents and made life hard for the poor but brought Chile prosperity. Pinochet himself passed power back to an elected president, but he kept his rank as army commander-in-chief, with immunity from the law for actions committed during his rule.

Ahmed Sukarno (1902–70) President of Indonesia 1945–67 A member of the anti-Dutch movement for Indonesian independence from its earliest days in the 1920s, Sukarno had an outstanding gift for languages and could move a mob to tears or frenzy in any of a dozen tongues. His great gift to his country was the creation of the modern Indonesian language, which united a nation of island-dwellers scattered over 5000 kilometres (3000 miles). As first president of an independent Indonesia, Sukarno's vanity led him to parade as a world statesman and waste Indonesia's natural wealth on grand projects which did nothing for the poor. Accused of corruption, he was overthrown by General Suharto (1921–), whose long period of military rule was even more corrupt, on an even greater scale. Suharto was driven into exile by a popular uprising in 1998.

Slobodan Milosevic (1941–) After a successful career as a Communist official, in 1988 Milosevic became President of Serbia, the most powerful part of Yugoslavia. His pro-Serb actions made him popular in Serbia but led Slovenia and Croatia to fight successfully for their independence. Milosevic encouraged Serb fighters in Bosnia to add lands under their control to Serbia and then used Serb forces against the Albanian inhabitants of Kosovo, causing thousands more deaths and a massive refugee crisis. Within Serbia he and his family abused their position to enrich themselves and used bribery, violence and rigged elections to stay in power. After his overthrow by opposition Serbs, Milosevic was handed over to an international tribunal at The Hague in 2001 and faced charges of war crimes and crimes against humanity.

Glossary

arbitrary acting on personal wishes, regardless of law or reason

authoritarian system of government that demands strict obedience, but does not try to control everything

caudillismo tradition of rule by a single dictator in Spanish-speaking countries

charismatic having extraordinary powers of personality

civilian person who is not a member of the army or police force

colony country ruled by another one

communism belief in a government based on the idea that a single ruling political party can run a country for the benefit all its peoples better than if they are left to make their own decisions and keep their own private homes, land and businesses

constitution set of rules setting out how a system of government should work

decree statement having the force of law

democracy system of government by the whole population. Voters usually elect representatives who govern the country

demonstration parade or mass-meeting in support of a cause

despot absolute ruler or tyrant

dictatorship rule by a single person or small group with complete power, not answerable to a parliament

exile living in another country for political reasons

fascism system of dictatorship which puts the nation before the individual and forbids opposition

guerilla member of a small armed group, fighting against a larger, regular army

ideology organized system of ideas to be put into practice through political action

junta Spanish word for a group of military officers who have seized power by force

legitimacy having the right to rule

literacy ability to read or write

massacre systematic killing of large numbers of people

militia a part-time armed force of volunteers

monarchy system of government in which a country is ruled by a king or queen

Nazi short name of the National Socialist German Workers' Party (Nationalsozialistiche Deutsche Arbeiterpartei), led by Adolf Hitler. The Nazis ruled Germany from 1933–1945. Nazism is the German form of fascism

pagan believer in pre-Christian gods

partisan armed volunteer fighter who is not part of a regular, professional army

patriot person who loves his or her country

post-colonial independent state which was once a colony

propaganda communication through messages and symbols aiming to persuade people to support a particular point of view, usually through appealing to emotion rather than reason

regime system or style of government

reprisals actions taken to punish attacks

republic country in which power is held by the people, or by their elected representatives, not by a monarch. A republic often has an elected president as head of state.

rule of law situation in which citizens are treated fairly, according to known rules applied equally to all

SA (Sturmabteilung) storm troopers: the Nazi Party militia

SS (Schutzstaffel) defence squadron: Hitler's personal bodyguard. The SS eventually grew into a Nazi party army with hundreds of thousands of members

sanctions limits on trade or other contacts to punish a country

secret police police, usually in civilian clothes, who operate in secret and outside the control of the law and court system, often using threats, torture and murder

secular non-religious

Slav person speaking one of the Slavonic languages such as Russian, Polish or Bulgarian

socialist person who believes in using government to make the lives of citizens more equal

Soviet Union the Union of Soviet Socialist Republics (USSR), a communist empire governed by Russia which lasted from 1922 to 1991

technocrat person with special skills of management, especially good at running large organizations

totalitarian type of dictatorship which aims at complete control over every aspect of people's lives

tyranny rule by an oppressive or cruel ruler, called a tyrant

Index

Afghanistan 18, 55
Albania 29, 50
Amin, Idi 12, 46
Argentina 10, 27, 30, 49, 59
armed forces 8, 16, 24, 27, 28, 29
Atatürk (Mustafa Kemal) 39–41
Austria 36, 38
authoritarian regimes 38, 50

Banda, Hastings 47
Bokassa, Jean-Bédel 45–6
Bolivar, Simon 26–7
Bolivia 26, 27
Borgia, Cesare 15
Brazil 49
Britain 24–5, 29
Burma 30

Caesar, Julius 22, 23
Caligula, Emperor 16
Cambodia 53–4
Castro, Fidel 43–5
caudillismo 10, 27
Ceausescu, Nicolae 43, 48
Chile 11, 27, 30, 49, 59
China 28, 55, 59
civilian dictatorship 12
colonialism 23, 27, 29
communism 9, 11, 18, 19, 28, 29, 31,
    44, 48, 49, 50, 51, 55
Cromwell, Oliver 22, 24–5
Cuba 43–5

De Gaulle, Charles 23
democracies 7, 9, 10, 40, 49
despots 13

Ethiopia 11

fascism 9, 10, 18, 19, 28, 31–4
France 23, 25–6, 29

Germany 4–5, 10, 19, 28, 34–8, 49, 55
Ghana 12, 30, 41–3
Greece 22, 39, 49, 55

Haiti 51
Hitler, Adolf 4–5, 6, 7, 9, 33, 34–8, 51,
    55
Hoxha, Enver 29, 50
Hungary 38
Hussein, Saddam 30, 52, 53, 54

Indonesia 30, 60
Iran 18, 41
Iraq 30, 52, 53
Islam 18, 40, 41
Italy 10, 13, 14, 15, 19, 28, 31–4

Key features of dictatorships 7, 55
Kim Jong-Il 51

Latin America 10, 26–7, 49
Libya 46, 52

Machiavelli, Niccolo 14–15
Malawi 47
Mao Zedong 6, 9, 28, 55
mass meetings and rallies 37, 53
Medici family 13, 15
Mexico 30, 49
military dictatorships 12, 24, 25, 27, 49
Mobutu, President 46–7
modern dictatorships 7, 13, 17, 22,
    31–54, 55
monarchies 12-13, 23, 32, 34, 55
Mussolini, Benito 8, 9, 19, 31, 32, 33,
    34, 37

Napoleon Bonaparte 22, 25–6
Nazism 4, 9, 19, 21, 28, 34, 35, 36, 38
new technologies 5, 17, 19, 27–8, 36
Nigeria 30, 49
Nineteen eighty-four (George Orwell)
    21
Nkrumah, Kwame 12, 30, 41–3
North Korea 51, 54

Pakistan 30, 49
Paraguay 27
Peru 49
Poland 36, 38, 49
Portugal 38
power, abuse of 7, 22, 23, 55

Qaddafi, Muammar al- 52, 54

religion 13, 14, 17, 18–19, 36, 38, 40
Romania 38, 43, 48, 49
Rome 22-3

Saudi Arabia 18, 46
Serbia 50, 55
Soviet Union 9, 19, 20, 21, 28, 29,
    44, 49, 55
Spain 10, 28, 30, 38, 49
Stalin, Joseph 6, 19, 20, 21, 33, 51
Syria 30, 50, 54